BACKYARD BOUNTY

Dorothy F. Weber

A POTPOURRI
OF PLEASURES AND TREASURES

by
Dorothy Fitzcharles Weber

BERGAMOT & BLACK EYED SUSANS

This journal is written in memory of my parents:
William Grant Fitzcharles,
Florence Sinclair Parker Fitzcharles
and my brother,
William Grant Fitzcharles, Jr.,
admirable gardeners.

ANOTHER BACK PORCH BOOK

This pictorial journal was inspired by my early exposures to plants and flowers as a very young child on "Greentrees Farm" in Pennington, New Jersey, where my father, William Grant Fitzcharles found frequent occasions in his busy schedule as merchant and gentlemen farmer to point out certain plants and flowers to his children.

We took many lovely spring walks in Howe's Woods or Kunkle Park to observe jack-in-the-pulpits, spring beauties and the rebirth of nature, including the birth of spring lambs on the farm.

I became fascinated with creating things from natural materials. This fascination was fueled by my father's inspirational love of nature and art.

My first creation at about age five, aside from daisy chains, was crushing ink berries to paint and write with, as our early native Americans had previously done.

While sitting absorbing nature in my own back yard, I have created leaf prints, wild vine and coiled pineneedle baskets.

Hence, I shall express in this little book the pleasures and treasures that I have derived from my backyard and others.

GREENTREES
My Family Home

This avian replica of the main house at "Greentrees" Farm is the creation of James Babbitt, grandson of William Fitzcharles, the restorer and owner of "Greentrees" from 1928 until 1985.

The original plantation parcel was deeded to Noah Van Kirk by his parents, John and Elizabeth Van Kirk, May 6, 1812.

GREENTREES BIRDHOUSE

The original survey was made in 1755. "...Beginning at a stone by a hickory stump corner of lands of said John Van Kirk and in Samuel Moore's line N 1° 15' W 25 chains* 56 links to a stone in the middle of the road leading from Pennington, New Jersey (originally Queenstown) to Stony Brook Bridge N 88° E 28 chains 82 links to a stone corner of Daniel Blackwell's land in Levi Ketcham's line, S 1° 15' E 25 chains 80 links, thence in Samuel Moore's line and corner to Daniel Blackwell, S 88° 45' W 28 chains 82 links to place of beginning.

Courtesy of Hopewell Valley Historical Society, Pennington, New Jersey.

*A surveyor's chain used throughout the years is a distance measuring device. There are 100 links in the measuring chain and it is 66 feet or 20 meters in length.

WHAT IS A GARDEN?

The word "gart" from old high German means "an enclosure."

Later, an old French word, "gardin" (now "jardin") developed.

Webster's Dictionary also says it is a plot of ground where herbs, fruit, flowers or vegetables are cultivated.

There are many similarities in the myriad of words representing "garden" in other languages.

A few examples are:

Italian — Giardino

Spanish — Jardin

Portuguese — Jardin

Latin — Hortus

Greek — Ykapdev

Gaelic — Garradh

Welsh — Gardd

Russian — Oropoa

Polish — Ogrod

Czechoslavakian — Zahrada

Chinese — Yuanzi

French — Jardin

Swedish — Tradgard

Dutch — Tuin

German — der Garten

From the Garden of Eden to the Hanging Gardens of Babylon to Monet's Garden at Giverny, down through the centuries to DuPont's Longwood Gardens, "a thing of beauty is a joy forever."

John Keats

"...And the Lord God planted a garden eastward in Eden."

My Eden

LOBLOLLY PINE

My garden is a shady retreat,
With ferns and primroses, it is replete.
Bluebirds, cardinals and an occasional jay
Set an idyllic pace on a day in May.
Pine needles lazily enact their descent
From trees not straight but so often bent.
They tend to create a muted sound
As they form a carpet on my ground.
Their fragrant aroma lends essence to the air —
Woodsy, cool, eternally there.

D.F. Weber

I will lead you...

CORAL BELLS

Along Garden

TURTLE

**DUTCH
IRIS
AND
DAISIES**

AMARYLLIS

My
Walk

ALIUM

MAY APPLE

The year's at the spring
And day's at the morn;
Morning's at seven;
The hill-side's dew-pearled;
The lark's on the wing;
The snail's on the thorn:
God's in His heaven —
All's right with the world!

by Robert Browning

BLEEDING HEART

The Daffodils

I wandered lonely as a cloud
That floats on high o'er vales and hills,
When all at once I saw a crowd,
A host of golden daffodils,
Beside the lake, beneath the trees
Fluttering and dancing in the breeze.

DAFFODIL ARRANGEMENT

Continuous as the stars that shine
And twinkle on the milky way,
They stretched in never-ending line
Along the margin of a bay:
Ten thousand saw I at a glance
Tossing their heads in sprightly dance.

The waves beside them danced, but they
Out-did the sparkling waves in glee:
A poet could not but be gay
In such a jocund company!
I gazed — and gazed — but little thought
What wealth the show to me had brought:

For oft, when on my couch I lie
In vacant or in pensive mood,
They flash upon that inward eye
Which is the bliss of solitude;
And then my heart with pleasure fills,
And dances with the daffodils.

William Wordsworth

CORAL HONEYSUCKLE

CORAL HONEYSUCKLE ARRANGEMENT

Coral honeysuckle may be cultivated or wild. It is a favorite of the hummingbird and supplies beautiful red fall berries.

A visit to George Washington's home, Mount Vernon, reveals these flowering vines adorning the arched walkway that connects the main house with the office.

Coral Honeysuckle

"to paint or gild the lily"

RUST LILIES

from

King John

Act IV

Scene II

by William Shakespeare

"*You can't pluck flowers without a few thorns.*"

Perry Tanksley

A GARDENER'S TOOLS

SUNDIAL

"*The day is done
   and darkness
Falls from the wings
   of Night,
As a feather is
   wafted downward
From an eagle in
   his flight.
Not, from the grand
   old masters
Whose distant
   footsteps echo
Through the
   corridors of time.*"

Henry Wadsworth Longfellow

ATTRACTING BEES

HOLLYHOCK OR ALTHEA

The Hollyhock was originally from China and conjures up images of an English cottage garden and honeybees.

Early American colonists crammed seeds into their baggage for memories of home and for new gardens in the colonies.

The aspiring plants were prevalent in early New England along picket fences and old stone walls.

The Hollyhock was known in ancient Greece and was utilized for medicine, a dye and for its plant fiber.

They reach for the sky and symbolize ambition and a liberal nature.

The seeds for my flowers were crammed into my baggage from Taos and Santa Fe, New Mexico and from a charming walled garden in Craighurst, Ontario.

Honey Bees...
The Gardener's Friends

Luther Burbank, a frontiersman in plant experimentation and development, found that bees and hummingbirds were his best friends.

He would plant rows of plants so situated that the bees and hummingbirds would invariably cross back and forth, dropping pollen from one flower to another.

BEE SKEP AND MINT

The honey bees who adored the hollyhock were housed in early herb gardens in handwoven skeps such as this one.

*"Lemon balm to
cheer the bee
Lemon balm
in fruits and
tea
Lemon balm
for
sympathy..."*

Elizabeth
Morse

The platforms on which bee skeps stood
were scoured with branches of lemon balm in the
seventeenth century to attract any errant swarm.
Today the beekeepers grow balm for its high
yield of nectar . . . rubbing fresh balm on
wooden furniture gives it a good gloss and
delicious fresh scent. The oils in the herb foliage
do the wood as much good as commercial
lemon oil polish.

*from "A Basket of Herbs"
by Tasha Tudor*

An old Virginia Tidewater
recipe calls for a bed of fresh
lemon balm placed under
seasoned fish fillets before
broiling.

A
Backyard
Tea Sampling

In order to dry herb leaves for tea, six stalks loosely tied together may be hung upside down in a dry cool place out of direct sunlight.

Another method is placing the individual leaves, that have been washed and patted dry, on a tray in a single layer and left to dry completely.

Lemon balm is a perenniel herb. It may be used fresh, frozen or dried in hot or cold tea.

"Mint — I am intoxicated by the fragrance."

Henry David Thoreau

Spearmint and peppermint are so refreshing for tea, lemonade and candies, and are truly "cool refreshment."

Mint was highly regarded in Biblical times and used in medieval homes, castles and monasteries. In ancient Rome, mint symbolized hospitality.

Bees love the lavender mint flowers and mint honey is a delicious addition to teas.

MINT ARRANGEMENT WITH RUSSIAN TEA SAMOVAR

Mint Honey

Add ¼ cup chopped fresh mint to 1½ cups honey.
Let mixture warm on low heat for 10 minutes.
After standing for 2 hours, remove the mint
leaves and store at room temperature.
Share some with a friend.

Peppermint Patch
Side Dish

To accompany lamb, poultry or seafood
Serves four

3 tender sprigs of peppermint
2 tablespoons nonfat yogurt
3 small cucumbers

Wash and peel the cucumbers; slice very thin.
Mix them into chopped mint and yogurt.
Garnish with a sprig of mint.

Peppermint, Applemint and Pineapple Mint
are a few that are favorites.

Steep several teaspoons of dried mint leaves
in boiling water for five minutes; strain and imbibe.

Planting your tea herbs outside the back door
in a sunny, well-drained area will make them
handy, attractive and aromatic.

Bee Balm or Bergamot

The bee balm, a truly native American wildflower, was introduced into the colonial garden after the Oswego Indians showed the colonists how to make tea from the dried leaves.

BERGAMOT

The showy flowers in shades of pink, lavender and red attract bees, hummingbirds and butterflies.

Bergamot petals are edible and make a lovely salad garnish.

The Violet

*"I know a bank where the wild thyme blows.
Where oxlips and the nodding violet grows."*

by William Shakespeare

Shakespeare's favorite flower, the violet, may be candied, eaten in salads, fruitcups or as a lovely edible decoration on white cake icing.

ANOTHER FAVORITE OF THE BEES

Violet Honey

½ cup violets
½ cup water
¼ cup honey
1 cup white wine

Mash the flowers and water with a mortar and pestle. Remove the flowers.

Combine the liquid with the honey and wine in a saucepan.

Bring this to a boil; cool down and store in a jar as an interesting sauce for ice cream.

> *"...I remember, I remember*
> *The violets, and the lily-cups —*
> *Those flowers made of light!*
> *The lilacs where the robin built,*
> *And where my brother set*
> *The laburnum on his birthday,*
> *The tree is living yet!"*
>
> Thomas Hood

A delightful quote from Elizabeth Chatsworth:

> *"Every year, on the day when Laura found the first violet, her mother made a layer cake and an upside-down pudding and celebrated the return of the first robin."*

And
More
Herbs...

Courtesy of
Nancy Thomas

"And God said, Behold I have given you every herb bearing seed which is upon the face of all the earth, and every tree, in which is the fruit of a tree yielding seed; to you it shall be for meat."

Genesis 1:29

Basil

Basil is an oriental plant. It is revered and shared by lovers in Italy.

Peasant girls place basil in their hair when they go to meet their sweethearts.

"The house surrounded by basil is blessed and all who cherish the plant are sure of heaven."

Alice Morse Earle

Basil Vinegar

1 cup white vinegar
6 sprigs fresh basil
2 red nasturtuim blossoms

Put all ingredients in an attractive bottle and place in a sunny window for two weeks, turning frequently.

Remove the sprigs and blossoms and enjoy delicate pink basil vinegar on your salads, plain or in a vinaigrette.

Basil Oil

1 pint olive oil
½ cup fresh basil leaves
1 garlic clove

Heat oil until warm. Put the leaves in a jar. Pour the warm oil in and let cool.

Cover the jar and store in a dark area and in two to three weeks strain and use in salad dressing or as a saute' for meats and stirfry vegetables.

Virginia Pesto
For Pasta, Chicken or Fish

2 cups washed and dried fresh basil leaves
    (stems removed)
2 garlic cloves, peeled and chopped
A scant ½ cup olive oil
3 heaping teaspoons of pecan meal
    (finely ground pecans)
1/3 to 1/2 cup parmesan cheese, grated

Put the garlic and basil in a blender. Add the olive oil. Blend until smooth. Stir in the pecans and cheese. Serve over penne or other pasta of choice. This may be frozen. It is best to put a small amount of oil on the top before freezing.

Sliced Tomatoes / Basil Salad

4 sliced tomatoes
2 tablespoons fresh basil leaves, chopped
  (or 2 teaspoons dry basil)
2 tablespoons olive oil

Sprinkle basil on the tomato slices, then pour on olive oil.

An interesting addition is very thin slices of mozarella cheese layered with the tomatoes.

Serve on salad plates, topped with a fresh basil sprig.

Lavender

Lavender Vinegar

Lavender vinegar is a lovely addition to bath water. Fill a pretty bottle with lavender sprigs and flowers too. Pour white vinegar to the top of the bottle.

Put on the lid and let it absorb sunshine on a windowsill.

After about 2 weeks, remove the flowers and sprigs and put in a fresh sprig.

Tie on an attractive ribbon and use as a gift for a friend, for a fragrant bathwater additive.

Lavender flowers are lovely dried to use alone or in a potpourri mixture.

Huge lavender growing farms are still in existence in Norfolk, England and are used for perfumes, soaps and sachets.

Parsley

Parsley is a lovely, edible garnish for soups, salads, casseroles and stews. It contains vitamin C and is excellent for digestion as related in Peter Rabbit's visit to Mr. McGregor's Garden.

"First he ate some lettuces and some French beans and then feeling rather sick, he went to look for some parsley."

PARSLEY IN MORTAR WITH PESTLE

Parsley and Chive Butter

3 tablespoons chopped parsley
3 tablespoons chopped chives
1 stick of softened butter

Mix and let stand overnight.
Delicious served on French or Italian bread.

Chives

A chive plant may be grown inside or outside. It is a perennial with a delicate onion-like flavor.

I have chopped it and frozen it for many culinary uses.

Twice Baked Potatoes With Chives

Select one more baking potato than the number of halves you plan to serve.

Wash them.

Dry them.

Rub the skins with a little butter or margarine.

Bake the potatoes until very soft at 400° F.

When the potatoes are cool enough to handle, cut them in half length-wise and scoop out the centers.

Combine the centers with enough milk to moisten well, a heaping tablespoon of butter, ¼ teaspoon of nutmeg, ⅛ teaspoon of black or white pepper and 1 tablespoon of chopped chives.

Beat all of this with an electric mixer and return this to the potato skins, heaping them full.

Sprinkle paprika on the tops and return to a 400° F oven until slightly browned.

These may be made in advance and heated and browned before serving.

The Nasturtium

The botanical name "tropaeolum" means "trophy." The leaf resembles a shield and her flower, a helmet.

*"It is thought the nasturtium flower
is superior to a radish in flavor
and is eat in salads or without."*

John Randolph,
Virginia Colonial Gentleman

The leaves are decorative, edible and have a tangy taste of cress, the family to which it belongs.

To Pickle Nasturtiums

...gather the berries full grown
but young, put them in a pot,
pour boiling salt and water on,
and let stand three or four days;
then drain off the water and
cover them with cold vinegar
and a few blades of mace and
whole grains of black pepper.

from: Mrs. Mary Randolph
Virginia Colonial Lady

These berries resemble capers
after pickling and are often used
as a garnish.

Nasturtium Butter

10 sliced flowers
1 stick butter, unsalted
Pinch of salt

Process in the blender. Serve
with muffins, croissants or
unusual bread.

Pineapple Sage

This herb is a tasty addition to meat, poultry or vegetable stuffings.

The leaves may be frozen for adding flavor to soups and stews in cold weather months.

The bright red blooms of fall give a natural dye to herbal vinegars.

Stuffed Pumpkin

Preheat oven to 300° F

1 medium size baking pumpkin

Wash, cut out top, scoop out seeds and pulp

Use your favorite stuffing of rice, bread, apples, celery, onions and/or sausage.

1/3 cup chopped pineapple sage

Add a small amount of margarine melted in ½ cup of very hot water. Mix together all of these ingredients and loosely stuff the pumpkin. Replace the top. Place it in a baking dish with a small amount of water. Put the dish on the lowest oven rack and bake for one hour. Watch carefully so that it does not burn. Serve this whole at the table and cut into individual wedges.

NATURE'S MOST BEAUTIFUL INSECT

The butterfly, like the bee, creates the illusion of a floating flower above our gardens and there are special ways to attract them.

Park Blaine's "Cedar Works" in Moorhead, Iowa makes a butterfly hibernation box of western red cedar.

The colorful blue butterfly silhouette tends to attract them as it has the ability to reflect ultra-violet light.

BUTTERFLY BOX

Attracting Butterflies
The Environment for your Butterfly Garden
Courtesy of Park Blaine

Becoming more and more popular in the private environment are butterfly gardens, gardening specifically to attract butterflies. Let alone the beauty that a flower garden affords us, there is the other benefit of learning from nature while viewing these delightful creatures. The flowers in a garden produce the nectar that is essential to butterfly existence.

Butterflies are an integral part of this ecosystem and there have already been several species made extinct by mans incredible ability to keep on building.

As invertebrates, butterflies are part of our ecosystem and help pollinate crops, play a critical role in all food chains, regulate plant abundance, control one another's numbers and indicate the health of our ecosystem. Real estate development, which is destroying our native woods, is in so doing, destroying our butterfly populations. Native woods have been a traditional hibernation site, with hollow trees, old wood piles, fallen timber, undergrowth and old wooden buildings being some of the favored sites in the developmental cycle of butterflies.

Butterflies are drawn to successful butterfly gardens by having the appropriate flora and fauna in your yard. Flower beds filled with asclepias tuberosa (butterfly weed), phlox, bluebells, columbine, wood poppies, buddleia (butterfly bush), trillium, wild geranium, crested iris, violets, larkspur, daisies, bleeding heart, shooting star, fire pinks, and Indian pinks, are to mention several of the plant life varieties found in successful butterfly gardens.

Butterfly gardening generally involves planting brightly colored, nectar rich flowers in a sunny location while also providing the correct larval food sources for their caterpillars. Larval food sources are dill, and parsley, sweetviolets, purslane, milkweed, marigolds, asters, clover, nettles, thistles, willows, dogbane, alfalfa, and sunflowers to mention but a few.

They appear to prefer certain colors and sometimes investigate purple flowers first and often shun white flowers altogether. Nectar content may be more important than color and your garden should be somewhat sheltered from the wind. Wet or muddy areas and some spoiled fruit from time to time will dramatically increase butterfly numbers.

There are ten different species of butterflies in the United States that hibernate in or near their normal habitat areas. They are the Compton Tortoise Shell, Milbert's Tortoise Shell, California Tortoise Shell, Green Comma, Gray Comma, Angel Wing-Satyr, Mourning Cloak, Hoary Coma (Zephyr), Question Mark, and the Red Admiral. Each of these insects seeks out crevices, holes, tree bark, wood piles or similar hiding spots in which to hibernate.

Migrating butterflies will lay their eggs wherever they find the proper plant populations. The eggs then become caterpillars, who after stuffing themselves silly, shed several layers of skin like a snake. The third and last stage is when the last skin hardens into a pupa. This pupa is called a chrysalis and hangs from twigs or branches until the final metamorphis takes place and the brightly colored butterflies creep from their shells. They must cling tightly to where they are until their fragile wings gain enough strength to carry them away. The insects body temperature must be at least 94 degrees before it can fly.

The butterfly hibernation box is used to encourage butterflies to remain in the proximity of the owners garden. It should be mounted about 4 feet off the ground, or about the height of the flowers in the flower garden and placed in an area around trees and preferably in the shade. To make the box habitable, loosely place materials such as natural tree bark or dried pine bark mulch in the box to allow easy entrance for the butterflies.

Butterfly Hibernation Boxes are not a recent occurrence. They were first used in Northern Ireland at the Drum Manor Butterfly Garden in the late 1960's, to establish a butterfly garden in Tyrone County. The Garden was designed to attract large populations of native butterflies, and allow naturalists and the public to observe them in their adult and developmental stages.

After reading this information, you can consider yourself in the top 10% of the population in knowing how the butterfly survives.

The Daisy

DAISIES WITH BUTTERFLY

A favorite flower of the butterfly is the daisy. The "Wizard of Horticulture," Luther Burbank's most successful cultivated flower was the Shasta Daisy. It was developed from the finest specimens of wild ox-eye daisies.

From early childhood, he preferred plants to toys and most probably developed this plant love from his mother's guidance at his home in Lancaster, Massachusetts.

"The Edison of Horticultural Mysteries"

Luther Burbank

At a young age, Luther moved to California where he could grow plants year round. One of his most amazing experiments was the removal of desert cacti spines to make the cacti edible fodder for cattle.

SAGUARO CACTUS

A Saguaro Cactus, native to the Sonoran Desert of Arizona, grows to a giant height and houses birds in the opening or boot shaped hole.

GARDEN

CROCODILE

**A
JAUNTY
GENT**

WHIMSEY

A DOVE WITH ZINNIAS

Courtesy of Nancy Thomas

**A
STAR
SPANGLED
BENCH**

Courtesy of Nancy Thomas

A FAMILIAR YULETIDE VISITOR AMID NARCISSUS AND EVERGREENS

by Patricia McDonald

THE HOUSE THAT JACK BUILT

Courtesy of Wild Birds Unlimited, Williamsburg, Virginia

Nearly one hundred and fifty years ago, Henry David Thoreau paddled a birchbark canoe through the white water of the Allegash in northern Maine.

This "House That Jack Built" adopts another attractive waterproof and useful whimsey from birchbark for today's garden songbirds.

These pine needle baskets were created by the author from the southern Loblolly Pine Tree carpet in her backyard in Williamsburg, Virginia.

The baskets are coiled and secured with raffia in the manner of the early woodland Indians.

The Indians sometimes used them as molds for clay pots.

The vine baskets have been woven with the abundant honeysuckle in her backyard.

**PINE
NEEDLE
BASKETS**

A Colonial Williamsburg pumpkin dons a
tricorn hat to usher in fall.

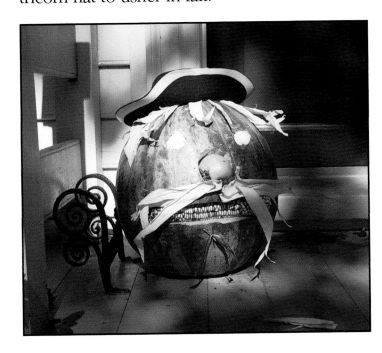

**PUMPKIN
WITH
TRICORN
HAT**

The headless farmer appears ready to run.

SCARECROW IN JEANS WITH CHRYSANTHEMUMS

Carved quail parade across the top of Sharon Lovejoy's "Hearts' Ease Gardens" in Cambria, California.

Sharon shares her whimsey with us.

Dear Dorothy,

...I live in a very rural area along the California coastline. My home garden is ½ acre of some terraced elevations filled with pines, oaks and native plants.

Large flocks of California quail shelter in my garden. I always provide plenty of seed and water for them and many of the bushes I've planted furnish them with berries.

The familiar chuckling and chortling and companionable scratchings of the quail contantly enfolds me. They are my friends and I love their presence.

When I started to install the gardens at "Hearts' Ease" in downtown Cambria, I said to an old friend, "There is only one thing missing from this garden - my quail." My friend, Bob Lennart (who is a fine woodworker) said, "I'll fix that!" and he proceeded to cut out (each one!!!) my quail-tipped picket fence to surround my garden and keep me company...

Sharon

From Our Mother Country

A FLOWER CART IN SOMERSET, ENGLAND
DECORATES A FOLK PARK

A true southern cabin that has been transported to the charming garden of Linda Dean at her shop "The Herb Cottage" in Bridgewater, Virginia. It was moved from her grandmother's property in Dayton, Virginia and was used as a washhouse. It is fine example of early Shenandoah Valley log construction.

KELLOGG HOMESTEAD BIRDHOUSE

In contrast to the log cabin, we find a replica of an early home in Mesa, Arizona.

A birdhouse for pioneer birds with all
the miniature necessities of a true
Conestoga Wagon, hangs in a
Shenandoah Valley snow scene at the
foot of the Blue Ridge Mountains,
awaiting adventurous spring occupants.

Courtesy of The Tom Linskis
of New Market, Virginia

"Gardeners Make The Best Bird Watchers"

"Each little flower that opens, each little bird that sings. He made their glowing colors, He made their tiny wings."

From All Creatures Great and Small

A PRIMITIVE BIRDTREE FROM PENNSYLVANIA IN THE AUTHOR'S COLLECTION

Randy Sewell of Muscogee Avenue in Atlanta, Georgia can always brighten your day with his original whimsical birdhouses that turn ordinary subjects into extraordinary creations.

JEWEL BOX WITH DIAMOND RING

JAVA JIVE WITH NEON

**IRONCLAD MONITOR
WITH LEAD DECK
AND GUN TURRET**

...and more of
Randy's avian
abodes.

**FEED SILO
WITH SUET CRIB**

ARRANGEMENTS

Twenty-five hundred years ago Plato said, "Nature is Divine Art." So begins my mother's commencement address entitled, "Nature Indoors."

It was presented at the 55th annual commencement on June 18, 1912, upon her (Florence Sinclair Parker's) graduation from the State Model School in Trenton, New Jersey. She further states: "Nature's laws are:

    1. Harmony in color
    2. Fitness of form to function
    3. Simplicity"

and following these three rules of hers for bringing nature indoors, they create a fitting introduction to this section on arrangements.

Nature Indoors

A visit to my daughter's home in Charlotte.

ANTIQUE BOWL WITH HANDPAINTED BIRD

Courtesy of Patricia McDonald

From Garden to Table

Antique Chinese Teapot as painted by
Max Weber in oil in 1925, titled "Still
Life with Chinese Teapot," a gift of Mrs.
John D. Rockefeller to the Museum of
Modern Art.

Yuletide in Colonial Williamsburg, Virginia

Tidewater Virginia favorites: The oyster whose shell is incorporated with artistic appeal.

The pineapple has served as a symbol of hospitality since early colonial days when the clipper ships brought highly valued fresh tropical fruits to the plantations along the James and York Rivers.

The pomegranate is the thick skinned, reddish berry of a tropical tree prized in the old world, about the size of an orange and can be easily dried for arrangements.

The Osage orange is a non-edible fruit of an ornamental American tree belonging to the mulberry family. It was named for the Osage Indians. The wood of the tree is hard and orange. The fruit has a greenish-yellow pebbled skin.

SOUTHERN MAGNOLIA . . . FOR THE BIRDS!

This is one of the southern gardener's favorites for seasonal arrangements. It has ten inch flowers with shiny laurel-type leaves, rusty stems and rusty shoots.

WILD BLACK-EYED SUSANS IN AN ANTIQUE PEWTER EWER

COREOPSIS, FERNS AND DAISIES ON A COFFEE TABLE

DUTCH IRIS AND DAISIES IN A SILVER VICTORIAN CAKE BASKET BESIDE THE RAILING

A TREE IN FALL LEAF

*"The planting of trees is
the least self-centered of
all that we do..."*

Thornton Wilder

Gingko - **Maidenhair Tree**

The Gingko is the lone survivor of a tree family that lived in temperate areas when dinosaurs were roaming our earth. It has been called a "living fossil" and did survive in mild, oriental areas because of no glaciers. Its fan-shaped leaf resembles that of the maidenhair fern. Botanists consider the Ginkgo the missing link between flowering plants and ferns which both reproduce from a female fruit. The fleshy, odiferous yellow fruit of the Gingko is sold for food in China and Japan and used as a special nut at weddings and banquets. The nut is the silver-white inside part of the fruit. Gingko means "silver fruit" in Chinese. It has been known to grow to heights of 100 feet and was introduced to America in about 1784 from England and from Asia previously.

Paper Mulberry - **White**

This mulberry is native to Asia and was introduced in colonial days to the Atlantic seaboard in an unsuccessful attempt to house silk worms for the silk industry. What a saving it would have been for colonial ladies and gentlemen's fine silk clothing! Today we only have the gnarled ancient trees in Colonial Williamsburg to bear witness to the attempt.

As the leaves have fallen, it is a good time to reflect and one reflection might be the myriad of names we have derived from nature's trees and flowers to adopt as our own...

FALLEN LEAVES

Rose	Myrtle	Ginger	Can you
Heather	Pansy	Flora	add to
Lily	Iris	Basil	this list?
Narcissus	Daisy	Forest	
Holly	Rosemary	Timothy	
Ivy	Viola	Olive	
Fern	Violet		

The Leaves Have Gone and So...
A Memory of Long Ago

Making Angels in the Snow

Maple Sugar on Snow
(A child's delight from Vermont)

Boil maple syrup until it forms a sticky coating when dropped upon a pan of very clean, fresh fallen snow.

Drizzle a small amount on at one time.

This is delicious with hot chocolate after building a snowman.

"While the earth remaineth seedtime and harvest, and cold and heat, and summer and winter, and day and night shall not cease."

Genesis 7:9

NATURE GOES TO SLEEP